IT'S TIME TO EAT CURRANTS

It's Time to Eat CURRANTS

Walter the Educator

Silent King Books
A WhichHead Entertainment Imprint

Copyright © 2024 by Walter the Educator

All rights reserved. No part of this book may be reproduced in any manner whatsoever without written per- mission except in the case of brief quotations embodied in critical articles and reviews.

First Printing, 2024

Disclaimer

This book is a literary work; the story is not about specific persons, locations, situations, and/or circumstances unless mentioned in a historical context. Any resemblance to real persons, locations, situations, and/or circumstances is coincidental. This book is for entertainment and informational purposes only. The author and publisher offer this information without warranties expressed or implied. No matter the grounds, neither the author nor the publisher will be accountable for any losses, injuries, or other damages caused by the reader's use of this book. The use of this book acknowledges an understanding and acceptance of this disclaimer.

It's Time to Eat CURRANTS is a collectible early learning book by Walter the Educator suitable for all ages belonging to Walter the Educator's Time to Eat Book Series. Collect more books at WaltertheEducator.com

USE THE EXTRA SPACE TO TAKE NOTES AND DOCUMENT YOUR MEMORIES

CURRANTS

It's time to eat a tiny treat,

It's Time to Eat
Currants

Little currants, sour and sweet.

So small and round, like drops of cheer,

A handful brings delight so near.

They grow on bushes, short and stout,

With berries red or black throughout.

Picked with care, these gems so fine,

Are packed with flavor every time.

You can eat them fresh, straight from the vine,

Or dried and chewy, both are divine!

Sprinkle them on your morning oats,

Or mix them in your favorite bakes and loaves.

Currants bring you vitamins too,

They help you grow, they're good for you!

Full of power, packed with zing,

A tiny fruit that does big things.

It's Time to Eat
Currants

In muffins, cakes, or in a stew,

There's so much currants love to do.

Their tangy taste makes snacks complete,

A little burst that can't be beat.

For lunch or snacks, they're easy to share,

Grab some currants and show you care.

Pop them in, one, two, three,

And let the flavor set you free!

They're nature's jewels, so bright and bold,

A treasure more than gems or gold.

Whether dried or fresh, they're always a win,

Currants are joy, from outside to within.

If you're feeling hungry, grab a few,

They're tasty, healthy, and good for you.

A tiny fruit with so much to give,

It's Time to Eat
Currants

Currants are the snack to help you live.

So next time you see this fruity surprise,

Let the currants delight your eyes.

Snack away with a happy grin,

It's time for currants, let's begin!

From bushes to bowls, they're such a treat,

Currants are berries that can't be beat.

So grab a handful, let's all dine,

It's Time to Eat
Currants

On these tiny fruits that taste divine!

ABOUT THE CREATOR

Walter the Educator is one of the pseudonyms for Walter Anderson. Formally educated in Chemistry, Business, and Education, he is an educator, an author, a diverse entrepreneur, and he is the son of a disabled war veteran. "Walter the Educator" shares his time between educating and creating. He holds interests and owns several creative projects that entertain, enlighten, enhance, and educate, hoping to inspire and motivate you. Follow, find new works, and stay up to date with Walter the Educator™

at WaltertheEducator.com

www.ingramcontent.com/pod-product-compliance
Lightning Source LLC
LaVergne TN
LVHW052011060526
838201LV00059B/3978